# THE
# BIG BOOK
# OF KIDS'
# JOKES

Kay Barnham and Sean Connolly

ARCTURUS

ARCTURUS

This edition published in 2016 by Arcturus Publishing Limited
26/27 Bickels Yard, 151–153 Bermondsey Street,
London SE1 3HA

Written by Sean Connolly and Kay Barnham
Edited by Joe Harris
Illustrations by Adam Clay and Dynamo Design
This edition produced by Lucy Doncaster

ISBN: 978-1-78599-812-6
CH001967US
Supplier 38, Date 0816, Print run 5696

Printed in Canada

# CONTENTS

Never mind a quiet snigger, it's time to laugh out loud!
You'll struggle to contain your roaring outbursts with the
jokes in this awesome collection!

If you like to laugh, then you'll love this book of themed gags!
We've included everything from classics to one-liners, silly shaggy
dog stories to the best spoof films, song and book titles you've
never heard of, plus many, many more.

So open up this giggle-filled treasure chest and make your friends and
family smile with over 1,000 eye-wateringly funny jokes!

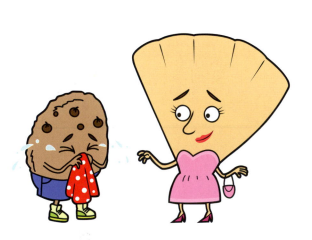

# ANIMAL ANTICS

**Why are dogs such bad dancers?**
They have two left feet.

**What's worse than raining cats and dogs?**
Hailing taxis.

**What happened to the cat that swallowed a ball of wool?**
She had mittens.

**How can you keep a wet dog from smelling?**
Hold its nose.

**Have you put some more water in the goldfish bowl?**
No. It still hasn't drunk the water I put in when I first bought it!

# ANIMAL ANTICS

Hey, you can't fish here, this is a private lake!
I'm not fishing, I'm teaching my pet worm to swim!

How do fleas get from one animal to another?
They itch hike!

What's the special offer at the pet store this week?
Buy one cat—get one flea!

What do you call a multistory pigpen?
A styscraper.

Why did the dog wear gloves?
Because it was a boxer.

My dog's a blacksmith.
How can you tell?
When I tell him off, he makes a bolt for the door.

Why did it take the Dalmatian so long to choose a vacation?
He was looking for just the right spot.

Why was the cat scared of the tree?
Because of its bark.

What animal wears a long coat in the winter and pants in the summer?
A dog!

What is a good pet for small children?
A rattlesnake!

**What type of dog can tell the time?**
A watchdog.

**How do you spell mousetrap using only 3 letters?**
C A T!

**Which pets are the noisiest?**
Trumpets!

**What did the dog say when it sat on some sandpaper?**
Ruff!

**Classified ad in local paper:**
"Dog free to good home—eats anything. Loves children!"

How do you stop a dog from barking in the back seat of a car?
Put it in the front seat.

What are dog cookies made from?
Collie-flour!

Johnny: Mom, is our dog metric?
Mom: Why do you ask?
Johnny: Because Dad said it has just had a liter of puppies!

Why did the dog limp into the Wild West saloon?
He came to find the cowboy who shot his paw!

I think I'm turning into a young cat.
You must be kitten me!

What do you call a cat that chases outlaws?
A posse cat!

What do you get if you cross an insect and a rabbit?
Bugs Bunny.

Did you hear about the well-behaved cat?
It was purrfect.

One boy says to another boy, "My pet's called Tiny."
"Why?" asks his friend.
"Because he's my newt."

Knock, knock!
Who's there?
Alf.
Alf who?
Alf feed the cat while you're on vacation!

What do cats drink in the desert?
Evaporated milk.

What do you call a column topped with a statue of
a famous cat?
A caterpillar!

What do you call a cat with eight legs?
An octopus.

What do you call a woman with a cat on her head?
Kitty.

What did the dog say when his owner stopped him from chewing the newspaper?
"You took the words out of my mouth!"

What do you get if you drop birdseed in your shoes?
Pigeon toes.

What did the clean dog say to the dirty dog?
Long time no flea!

My dog is a real problem. He chases anything and everything on a bike. I don't know what to do.
Just take his bike away!

**Which cats are great at bowling?**
Alley cats.

**What sort of dog is good at looking after children?**
A baby setter.

**Doctor, I think I'm a cat!**
How long have you felt like this?
**Since I was a kitten!**

**What do you get if a cat sits on a beach at Christmas?**
Sandy claws!

**First cat: Where do fleas go in the winter?**
Second cat: Search me!

# ANIMAL ANTICS

What happened to the Scottish cat who ran into the road without looking?
It was kilt!

How do you find a lost dog?
Make a sound like a bone!

Teacher: Can you define "dogmatic"?
Pupil: Is it a robot pet?

Did you hear about the cat who sucked a lemon?
He was a sourpuss.

What's a horse's favorite sport?
Stable tennis.

# ANIMAL ANTICS

**What's the difference between a well-dressed gentleman and an exhausted dog?**
One wears an expensive suit and the other just pants.

**Doctor, I feel as sick as a dog.**
I'll make an appointment for you to see a vet!

**Mom: Did you put the cat out?**
Kid: I didn't need to. It wasn't on fire!

**What do you use to clean a cat's hair?**
A catacomb.

**What do you give a sick parakeet?**
Tweetment!

**Why was the pig covered in ink?**
Because it lived in a pen.

**Why do pigs make terrible drivers?**
They're all road hogs.

**How do you make a cat happy?**
Send it to the Canary Islands!

**What do you call the place where cats and dogs go to get new tails?**
A retailer!

**What do you call a dog who is always rushing around?**
A dash-hound!

Where do you buy baby birds?
At the chickout.

What do you get if you leave a parrot cage open?
A polygon.

What do you get if you cross a honeydew and a sheepdog?
A melon collie.

Doctor, I think I'm a dog.
Well, take a seat and I'll have a look at you.
I can't—I'm not allowed on the furniture!

Did you hear about the boy who spilled spot remover on his dog?
The dog vanished.

**Why did the chicken sit on an ax?**
She wanted to hatchet.

**What did the traffic officer put on the car outside the dog kennel?**
A barking ticket.

**What's a dog's favorite hobby?**
Collecting fleas.

**What does your pet snake become if he gets a government job?**
A civil serpent!

**Why did the cat say "woof"?**
It was learning a foreign language.

**What do you get when you cross a parrot and a cat?**
A carrot

# ANIMAL ANTICS

**Where do huskies train for dogsled races?**
In the mushroom.

**Why did the dogs jump in the lake?**
To catch a catfish.

**What type of pet just lies around doing nothing?**
A carpet.

**Why did the dog chase his own tail?**
He was trying to make ends meet.

**Which dog wears a white coat and looks through microscopes?**
A lab!

**What do you call a prisoner's parakeet?**
A jail bird!

**Why did the cat pounce on the computer?**
Because he saw a mouse.

**What's happening when you hear "Meow—splat! Woof—splat!"**
It's raining cats and dogs.

**What has more lives than a cat?**
A frog—it croaks every night.

**Did you hear about the cat who drank three saucers of water in one go?**
She wanted to set a new lap record!

**Doctor, I feel like a dog!**
Sit!

**Why do dogs wag their tails?**
Because no one else will do it for them.

**What's red
and green and
jumps out of planes?**
A parrot-trooper!

**Why did the Dalmatian go to the eye doctor?**
He was seeing spots.

**What did Shakespeare's cat say?**
"Tabby or not tabby..."

**Why do dogs run in circles?**
Because it's hard to run in squares.

**What do you get when you cross a dog with a sheep?**
A sheep that can round itself up.

**What did the cowboy say when the bear ate his hunting hound?**
Doggone!

**What do parakeets wear to the beach?**
Beakinis.

**What happens when cats fight?**
They hiss and make up.

**What do you call rabbits marching backward?**
A receding hare-line.

What do you call a hamster who can pick up an elephant?
Sir!

What does a cat say when it is hurt?
Mee-OW!

How did the puppy stop the DVD player?
He used paws.

What do you get when you cross a dog with an elephant?
A really nervous mailman.

# ANiMAL ANTiCS

**Why are dogs longer at night than during the day?**
Because they are let out in the evening and taken in in the morning.

**What do you get if you mix a bird, a car, and a dog?**
A flying carpet.

**What kind of cat keeps the grass short?**
A lawn meower.

**Cat bumper sticker:**
"Life is hard—then you nap."

**What kind of bird does construction work?**
A crane.

Did you hear about the pig who walked around
the world?
He was a globetrotter.

Why is it called a "litter" of puppies?
Because they mess up the whole house.

What happened when the dog went to the flea circus?
He stole the show!

What did one flea say to the other flea?
"Should we walk or take the dog?"

# FUNNY FOOD

# FUNNY FOOD

**Why did the cookie cry?**
Because his mom had
been a wafer
so long.

**When do truck drivers stop for a snack?**
When they see a fork in the road.

**What did one plate say to the other plate?**
Lunch is on me.

**Knock knock.**
Who's there?
**Cash.**
Cash who?
**No, thanks. I prefer walnuts.**

**Why did the rhubarb go out with a prune?**
Because he couldn't find a date.

# FUNNY FOOD

This coffee is disgusting—it tastes like mud.
I'm not surprised—it was ground a few minutes ago!

Why did the chef serve frozen steak?
He wanted it to melt in the mouth.

What do you get if you cross a comedian and an orange?
Peels of laughter.

What do you call an airplane passenger covered in salt and pepper?
A seasoned traveler.

What did the speedy tomato say to the slow tomato?
Ketchup!

# FUNNY FOOD

**What happened at the cannibals' wedding?**
They toasted the bride and groom.

**Waiter, waiter, there's a button in my lettuce.**
Ah! That will be from the salad dressing, sir!

**Why did the man eat yeast and furniture polish
for breakfast?**
He wanted to rise and shine.

**Knock knock.**
Who's there?
**Arthur.**
Arthur who?
**Arthur any cookies left?**

**How do you make
a fruit punch?**
Give it boxing lessons.

**Why did the girl stare at the orange juice carton?**
Because it said "concentrate" on the label.

**Why was the chef so relaxed?**
He had plenty of thyme on his hands!

**What's yellow and dangerous?**
Shark-infested custard.

**Waiter, waiter—there's a fly in my soup!**
Sorry, madam, I didn't know you were vegetarian!

**Did you hear about the Thanksgiving turkey who tried to escape the roasting pan?**
He was foiled.

What do you get if you cross a Shakespeare play with an egg?
Omelet!

How do you know when a cannibal feels like eating you?
He keeps buttering you up!

What did the fat man say when he sat down at the dinner table?
"Just think—all this food is going to waist!"

How do you make golden soup?
Put 14 carrots in it!

What do you get if you divide the circumference of a pumpkin by its diameter?
Pumpkin pi.

A pizza walks into a bar and asks for a burger.
"I'm sorry," says the barman.
"We don't serve food."

Chef: I didn't use a recipe for this casserole—I made it up out of my own head!
Customer: I thought it tasted of sawdust!

If I cut a potato in two, I have two halves. If I cut a potato in four, I have four quarters. What do I have if I cut a potato in sixteen?
French fries!

Why did the bakers work late?
Because they kneaded the dough!

How much did the pirate pay for his corn?
A buck an ear.

**Waiter, can I have my lunch on the patio?**
Certainly, sir, but most people find a plate more sensible!

**Why should you never tell secrets in a corn field?**
Because you would be surrounded by ears!

**What farm animal can you spread on toast?**
A baby goat—it's a little butter!

**What's the most expensive item on the menu at a Chinese restaurant?**
Fortune cookies.

**Mmmmm! This cake is lovely and warm!**
It should be; the cat's been sitting on it all afternoon!

**What do computer operators eat for a snack?**
Chips!

**How do they eat their chips?**
One byte at a time.

**Which snack is wicked and lives in the desert?**
The sand witch!

**How do you keep flies out of your kitchen?**
Move the pile of rotting vegetables into the living room!

**What starts and ends with "t," and is also full of "t"?**
A teapot.

**What kind of bird is at every meal?**
A swallow.

Why did the vampire always carry a bottle of tomato ketchup?

He was a vegetarian!

What is the one thing that stays hot in the refrigerator?

Mustard!

What did the chewing gum say to the shoe?

I'm stuck on you.

Why did the beet blush?

Because he saw the salad dressing.

Knock knock.

Who's there?

Phil.

Phil who?

Phil this cup with sugar, would you, I've run out!

## FUNNY FOOD

**What do you get if you boil up 25 cars, three buses and a truckload of sugar?**
Traffic jam.

**Why is cutting a slice of gingerbread the easiest job in the world?**
It's a piece of cake.

**What is the best time to pick apples?**
When the farmer is away on vacation!

**Customer: Why is there a dead fly in my soup?**
Waiter: Well, you surely don't expect to get a live one at these prices!

**What did one snowman say to the other snowman?**
Smells like carrots.

## FUNNY FOOD

Why did the man send his alphabet soup back?
Because he couldn't find words to describe it!

Did you hear about the silly farmer who took his cows to the North Pole, thinking he would get ice cream?

Waiter—there's half a dead cockroach in my food!
You'll have to pay for the half you've eaten, sir!

How do you eat your Thanksgiving turkey?
I just gobble it down!

Did you hear about the eggs who kept playing tricks on people?
They were practical yolkers.

Why do bees have icky,
sticky hair?
They use honeycombs.

Waiter—this crab only has
one claw!
Sorry, sir, it must have been in a
fight!
In that case, take it away and bring
me the winner.

Doctor, I think I've just swallowed a chicken bone!
Are you choking?
No, I'm serious!

What do you call a lazy baker?
A loafer!

Waiter, this omelet tastes awful!
Sir, I can assure you that our chef has been making
omelets since he was a child!
That may be true, but can I have one of his fresher ones
please?

**Why did the lemon refuse to fight the orange?**
Because it was yellow!

**There's a stick insect in my salad—fetch me the branch manager at once!**

**Where is the best place to keep a pie?**
Your tummy!

**What type of lettuce did they serve on the Titanic?**
Iceberg.

# FUNNY FOOD

**Did you hear about the paranoid potatoes?**
They kept their eyes peeled for danger.

**Why do basketball players love donuts?**
They can dunk them.

**Why are seagulls called seagulls?**
Because if they flew over bays, they would be bagels.

**What did the carrot stick say to the potato chip?**
"Want to go for a dip?"

**What sort of dog has no tail?**
A hot dog!

# FUNNY FOOD

What do trash collectors eat?
Junk food.

Teacher: Sally, give me a sentence with the word "aroma" in it!
Sally: My uncle Fred is always traveling; he's aroma!

Teacher: Philip, why do you have a lunchbox in each hand?
Philip: It's important to have a balanced diet, Mr Harrison!

What do you get if you mix birdseed with your breakfast cereal?
Shredded tweet.

What is worse than finding a worm in your apple?
Finding half a worm in your apple!

**What's a cannibal's favorite take out?**
Pizza with everyone on it.

**What did the golfer eat for lunch?**
A sand wedge.

**Why are clocks greedy?**
They always have seconds.

**Why couldn't Batman go fishing?**
Because Robin had eaten all the worms.

**Did you hear about the strawberry who attended charm school?**
He became a real smoothie.

**Which part of Swiss cheese is the least fattening?**
The holes!

**What do you call a pig who does karate?**
A pork chop.

**Why did the potato cry?**
Its peelings were hurt.

**How do you make a stiff drink?**
Put cement in your cup.

**Did you hear about Professor Cole, the scientist who discovered the perfect ratio for mixing cabbage, carrot, onion, and mayonnaise?**
He called it Cole's Law.

**Why did the girl disappear into the bowl of granola?**
A strong currant pulled her under.

# FUNNY FOOD

Knock knock.
Who's there?
Police.
Police who?
Police can I have a chocolate milkshake?

What kind of nut always has a cold?
A cashew!

What do you call a fake noodle?
An impasta.

Johnny! How many more times do I have
to tell you to keep away from the
cookie jar?
No more times—
it's empty!

What do you get if you
cross a chicken with a
cement mixer?
A bricklayer.

# FUNNY FOOD

Does Dracula's chef ever cook roast beef?
Yes, but very rarely.

What is a chicken's favorite dessert?
Layer cake!

Knock knock.
Who's there?
Anita.
Anita who?
Anita nother hot dog—I'm starving!

How do you fix a broken
pizza?
With tomato paste!

Why did the man
wear a
banana skin
on each foot?
He wanted a
pair of
slippers.

Where do ghosts swim?
In the Dead Sea.

What did the vampire doctor say?
Necks please!

Did you hear about the banshee who wanted to be an actress?
She did a scream test.

What does a dragon call knights in armor?
Canned food!

**What do you get if you cross a vampire with a circus entertainer?**
Someone who goes straight for the juggler!

**What do you get if you cross a vampire with a mummy?**
Something you wouldn't want to unwrap!

**What do ghosts eat for dinner?**
Goulash!

**How do ghosts begin business letters?**
"Tomb it may concern…"

**Why didn't the skeleton fight the monster?**
He didn't have the guts!

**What has a pointy hat, a broomstick, and a blue face?**
A witch holding her breath.

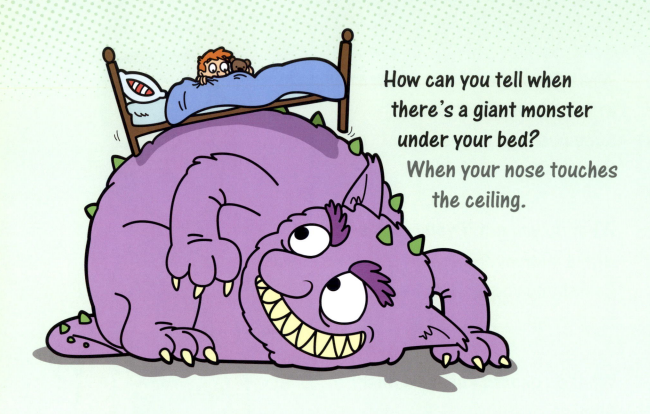

How can you tell when there's a giant monster under your bed?
When your nose touches the ceiling.

**What happened to the vampire with bad breath?**
His dentist told him to gargoyle twice a day!

**What do vampires do at eleven o'clock every night?**
They have a coffin break.

**What was written on the robot's gravestone?**
Rust in pieces!

**How does Frankenstein's monster sit in a chair?**
Bolt upright!

# MONSTER FUN

How do you know that smoking is harmful to your health?
Well, look what happened to all the dragons!

Should monsters eat people on an empty stomach?
No, they should eat them on a plate!

What is a monster's favorite party game?
Swallow the leader!

Why don't skeletons sing church music?
They have no organs.

What goes "WOO-HA-HA" THUMP?
Frankenstein's monster laughing his head off.

What job does Dracula have with the Transylvanian baseball team?

He looks after the bats!

Why do ghosts never feel guilty?

They have a clear conscience!

First friend: Did you know that you can get fur from a vampire?

Second friend: Really? What kind of fur?

First friend: As fur away as possible!

Why do vampires dislike computers?

They hate anything new-fang-led!

Why did the car stop when it saw the monster truck?

It had a nervous breakdown.

Why was young Dr. Frankenstein so popular?
Because he was great at making new friends!

How did you know I was a ghost?
Oh, I can see right through you!

How did the ghostly teacher make sure his pupils had learned what he had written on the board?
He went through it again!

Why did the monster buy an ax?
Because he wanted to get a-head in life!

How do vampires get clean?
In a blood bath!

**Why wasn't the werewolf astronaut allowed to land his spaceship?**
Because the moon was full!

**Who do vampires invite to their birthday parties?**
Anybody they can dig up!

**Why did Dracula advertise for a housekeeper?**
He wanted some new blood in the house!

**Who is the world's scariest superhero?**
Vampire bat-man!

**What sort of telescope lets you see ghosts?**
A horrorscope!

**What do you call a lazy skeleton?**
Bone idle!

**What did Frankenstein do when the monster's head kept falling off?**
He made a bolt for it!

**Why do monsters like to stand in a ring?**
They love being part of a vicious circle!

**Where do werewolves live?**
In warehouses.

**Why doesn't Dracula have any friends?**
Because he's a pain in the neck!

**What does Dracula drink?**
"De-coffin-ated" coffee!

"Hurry up," said the father skeleton to his son, "or you'll be late for the skull bus!"

What do you call a kind, helpful monster who likes flowers and butterflies?
A failure!

What did the old vampire say when he broke his teeth?
Fangs for the memory...

What does it say on the mummy's garage entrance?
Toot, and come in!

# MONSTER FUN

**Who was the winner of the headless horse race?**
No one. They all finished neck and neck!

**Why are you throwing garlic out of the window?**
To keep vampires away.
**But there aren't any vampires here.**
See—it works!

**Why did the giant robot feel sick after eating a train?**
He caught a commuter virus!

**If having hairy palms is the first sign of turning into a monster, what is the second?**
Looking for them!

**Why did Godzilla stop eating buildings?**
He got atomic ache!

**What do ghosts do if they are afraid?**
Hide under a sheet!

**Why did the monster have twins in his lunchbox?**
In case he felt like seconds!

**Why didn't the vampire laugh at the joke about the wooden stake?**
He didn't get the point!

**Why did the werewolf swallow a bag full of cents?**
Because he thought the change would do him good!

**Why do zombies always look so tired?**
They are dead on their feet!

**What is the first thing a monster eats when he goes to a restaurant?**
The waiter!

**What do monsters call a crowded swimming pool?**
Soup!

**Why did the robot need a manicure?**
He had rusty nails!

**Why didn't the phantom win the lottery?**
He didn't have a ghost of a chance!

**Why do football teams have to practice so much when they play against zombies?**
Because they face stiff competition!

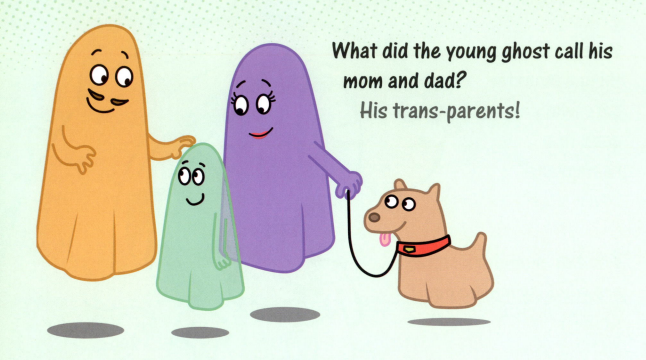

What did the young ghost call his mom and dad?
His trans-parents!

Why do little monsters not mind being eaten by ghosts?
Because they know they will always be in good spirits!

Why are there more ghost cats than ghost dogs?
Because every cat has nine lives!

Why do monster parents tell their children to eat cabbage?
Because they want them to have a healthy green complexion!

**Which monster is the most untidy?**
The Loch Mess Monster!

**Why did the cyclops school close down?**
Because they only had one pupil!

**Why are vampires stupid?**
Because blood is thicker than water!

**Why do other monsters find mummies vain?**
They're so wrapped up in themselves.

**Why do vampires never invite trolls to their dinner parties?**
They can't stand all that goblin!

**What do you call a ghostly chicken?**
A poultry-geist.

**Why did the zombie go to the drugstore?**
He wanted something to help stop his coffin.

**What do you call a child vampire?**
A pain in the knee!

**Who do vampires invite to their weddings?**
All their blood relatives!

How does a skeleton know
when it's going to rain?
He just gets a feeling in his
bones!

Why don't ghosts do aerobics?
Because they don't want to be
exorcised!

Why are owls so brave at night?
Because they don't give a hoot for
ghosts, monsters, or vampires!

How do vampires show affection for
each other?
They bat their eyelids!

What is the first thing you should put into a
haunted house?
Someone else!

Why did Goldilocks go to Egypt?
She wanted to see the mummy bear!

What did the werewolf say to the skeleton?
It's been so nice getting to gnaw you!

Why did the ghost go to the bicycle shop?
He needed some new spooks for his front wheel!

What do you get if you cross the Abominable Snowman with Count Dracula?
Severe frostbite!

What did the witch call her baby daughter?
Wanda!

What do you need to pick up a giant's silverware?
A forklift.

# MONSTER FUN

What do you call a male vampire in women's clothing?
Drag-cula!

How do you make a skeleton laugh?
Just tickle his funny bone.

Knock knock!
Who's there?
Russia!
Russia who?
Russia way——a monster's coming!

Why was the genie in the lamp angry?
Someone rubbed him up the
wrong way!

What do you get if you cross a warlock with a laptop?
A computer wizard!

What do skeletons say before eating?
Bone appetit!

What do you call the jewels that ghosts wear?
Tombstones!

What do dinosaurs rest their teacups on?
Tyrannosaucers.

How do you help Frankenstein's monster?
Give him a hand when he needs it!

How do witch children listen to stories?
Spellbound!

How can you tell
when a robot
is angry?
It flips its lid!

What flavor drink do
monsters slurp?
Lemon and slime.

Book spotted in the school library:
*The Haunted House* by Hugo First.

What do you call a hairy monster who's lost
his way home?
A where-am-I wolf.

**What happens when a witch catches the flu?**
Everyone gets a cold spell!

**Why do vampires have a steady nerve?**
They are as ghoul as cucumbers!

**Why don't vampires write their own books?**
They prefer to use ghost writers!

**Where do monsters like to go on vacation?**
Death Valley!

**Where do you find black holes?**
In black socks.

**What makes you think my son could be an astronaut?**
He has nothing but space between his ears!

**Did you hear about the woman who went in for plastic surgery, and came out looking like a Martian?**
She told the surgeon she wanted to look like a million dollars, so he made her face all green and crinkly!

**Which weighs the most, a full moon or a half moon?**
A half moon, because a full moon is much lighter!

**How do you get a baby astronaut to sleep?**
Rocket.

Knock knock.
Who's there?
Jupiter.
Jupiter who?
Jupiter spaceship
on my lawn?

Teacher: William,
how fast does light
travel?
William: I don't
know—it's already
arrived by the time
I wake up!

Which is the most glamorous planet?
Saturn. It has a lot of rings.

When can you be sure that the moon won't eat you?
When it's a full moon.

What crazy bug lives on the moon?
The lunar tick.

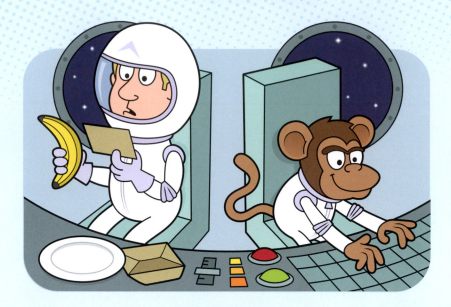

An astronaut and a chimp were fired off into space. The chimp opened its sealed orders, read them, and immediately started programming the flight computer. The astronaut opened his sealed orders and found only one instruction:

"Feed the chimp!"

**How do aliens go fishing?**
With Earthworms!

**What's the center of gravity?**
The letter V.

**Why do little green men have nice, warm homes?**
Because they live in little greenhouses!

**Why didn't the astronaut get burned when he landed on the sun?**
He went there at night!

**Why are parties on the moon always so dull?**
There's no atmosphere.

**Why do astronomers always bang their heads?**
It helps them to see stars!

**Book spotted in the school library:**
*Is There Life on Mars?* by Howard I. No.

**Three badly made robots were playing cards.**
The first one threw his hand in.
The second one rolled his eyes.
The third one laughed his head off.

**Why don't astronauts keep their jobs for long?**
Because after their training they're always fired.

**What did one rocket say to the other?**
I wish I could quit smoking!

**Some meteorites collide with planets. What do you call meteorites that miss?**
Meteowrongs.

**Why did the alien turn the restaurant staff upside down?**
Someone told him that you had to tip the waiter!

**What did one asteroid say to the other asteroid?**
"Pleased to meteor."

**What do aliens cook their breakfasts on?**
Unidentified frying objects.

**What do young astronauts sit on during takeoff?**
Booster seats.

**How does the solar system hold up its pants?**
With an asteroid belt.

**What did the boy star say to the girl star?**
Do you want to glow out with me?

**Why did the alien build a spaceship from feathers?**
He wanted to travel light years!

**What is an alien's favorite type of snack?**
A Martian-mallow.

Why do astronauts have to prepare a meal before blastoff?
They get hungry at launch time.

Why do astronauts make good football players?
They know how to make a great touchdown!

Why was the thirsty astronaut loitering near the computer keyboard?
He was looking for the space bar.

Big alien: If this planet is Mars, what's that one over there?
Little alien: Is it Pa's?

**What did the metric alien say to the human?**
"Take me to your liter."

**Did you know that they have found life on another planet?**
Really?
**Yes, there are fleas on Pluto!**

**What holds the moon up?**
Moon beams.

**Why is an alien such a good gardener?**
Because he has two green thumbs.

**Why are grandma's teeth like stars?**
Because they come out at night.

**Where do you leave your spaceship when you visit another planet?**
At a parking meteor!

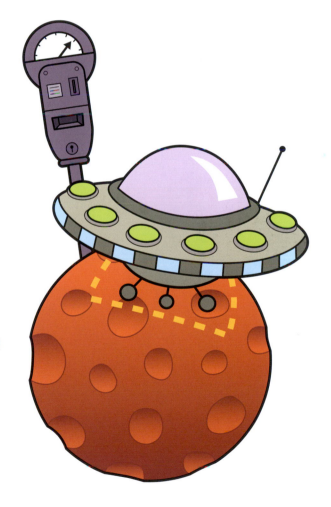

**Why do cats hate flying saucers?**
Because they can't reach the milk!

**What's an astronomer?**
A night watchman with a college education.

**Which actor won the Martian Oscars?**
Kevin Outer-Spacey!

**Why do astronauts never diet?**
No one needs to lose weight in space, because everything is weightless!

**Why did the spaceship land outside my bedroom?**
You must have left the landing light on!

**What's an alien's favorite drink?**
Gravi-tea.

**What did Saturn say when Jupiter asked if he could call him?**
"Don't call me—I'll give you a ring."

**What's normal eyesight for a Martian?**
20-20-20!

**What should you do if you see a spaceman?**
Park your car in it, man!

**I don't know what to buy my pal, the space alien, for his birthday.**
How about five-and-a-half pairs of slippers?

**What does an alien gardener do with his hedges?**
Eclipse them every spring!

**Why did the alien launch a clock into space?**
He wanted to see time fly.

**How did the alien tie his shoelaces?**
With an astro-knot.

**Why don't aliens celebrate each other's birthdays?**
They don't like to give away their presents.

**What's faster than the speed of light?**
The speed of dark!

**Who is a robot's favorite cartoon character?**
Tin-tin!

**When is a window like a star?**
When it's a skylight.

**If an athlete gets athlete's foot, what does an astronaut get?**
Missile toe!

**What is woolly and comes from outer space?**
A ewe-F-O.

How did the aliens hurt the farmer?
They landed on his corn.

What do you call an overweight alien?
An extra-cholesterol.

First astronomer: Do you think there's intelligent life out there?
Second astronomer: I doubt it. All the aliens I've met are pretty stupid!

Why did the robot go crazy?
He had a screw loose.

Why couldn't the alien's spaceship travel at the speed of light?
Because he took off in the dark!

**What do you call a sick space monster?**
An ailin' alien.

**Spotted on the science shelf of the school library:**
*Fly Me to the Moon*
by Tay Cough

**Why did the boy become an astronaut?**
Because his teacher told him he was no Earthly good.

**Why are astronauts such successful people?**
They always go up in the world.

**Which is more useful, the sun or the moon?**
The moon—because it shines at night when you want the light. The sun shines during the day, when you don't really need it!

**What did the alien say to the gas pump?**
*"Don't you know it's rude to stick your finger in your ear when I'm talking to you?"*

**I've given up on time travel.**
*Why?*
**There's no future in it.**

**Living on Earth may be expensive—but it does include a free trip around the sun each year.**

**Why are there no Martian tourists at the Grand Canyon?**
*Because it looks so much like home!*

How do you phone the sun?
You use a sun-dial.

Mars got sent to prison after the big robbery trial.
Why? He wasn't even there!
Yes, but he helped to planet.

What is a light year?
The same as a normal year,
but with fewer calories.

What did the astronaut say to his
alien girlfriend?
"You're out of this world!"

What do astronauts wear
in bed?
Space jammies.

How do aliens stay clean?
They take meteor showers.

What is an alien's favorite board game?
Moon-opoly!

How do astronauts serve drinks?
In sunglasses.

How do aliens keep from falling over in a spaceship?
They Klingon.

Why do astronauts find it hard to mix with other people?
They're not really down to Earth.

Why does Superman wear such big shoes?
Because of his amazing feats.

Clones are
people, two.

Have you seen the movie about
toads in space?
It's called Star Warts.

What is an astronaut's favorite music?
Rocket and roll.

Did you hear about the resentful robot?
He had a microchip on his shoulder.

What should you do if you meet a little green man?
Come back when he's a little riper.

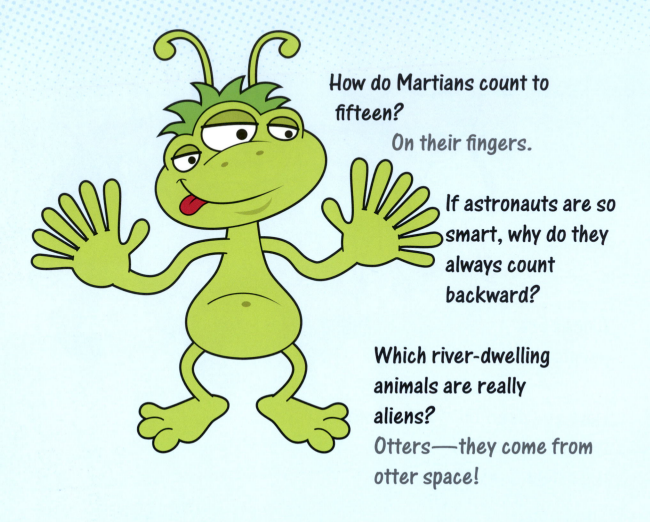

How do Martians count to fifteen?
On their fingers.

If astronauts are so smart, why do they always count backward?

Which river-dwelling animals are really aliens?
Otters—they come from otter space!

How many Martians does it take to screw in a light bulb?
Millions! One to hold the bulb, and the rest to turn the planet.

What did the loser in the astronomy contest receive?
The constellation prize.

# SCHOOL'S COOL

**What was the dentist's favorite subject at school?**
Flossophy.

**What did the number 0 say to the number 8?**
"That's a cool belt."

**What do you get if you cross a vampire with a teacher?**
Blood tests.

**Why did the teacher wear sunglasses?**
Because his class was so bright.

**Why did the teacher jump into the swimming pool?**
He wanted to test the water.

What kind of lunches do geometry teachers enjoy?
Square meals.

Principal: You'll start with a salary of $25,000 and then go up to $35,000 in six months.
Teacher: In that case I think I would like to start in six months!

Why was the cross-eyed teacher's class rioting?
She couldn't control her pupils.

Why was the broom late for school?
It overswept.

Teacher: Who invented King Arthur's round table?
Pupil: Was it Sir Cumference?

Did you hear about the cannibal who was expelled from school?
He was buttering up the teachers.

Teacher: What language do they speak in Cuba?
Pupil: Cubic!

Why did one pencil tell the other pencil it looked old and tired?
Because it was blunt.

What's the tastiest class at school?
History. It's full of dates.

**My music teacher said I have a heavenly voice!**
That's not strictly true—she said your voice was like nothing on Earth!

**Teacher: You missed school yesterday, didn't you?**
Pupil: Not very much!

**What sum do math teachers like best?**
The summer.

**Teacher: Why are you taking that sponge into class?**
Pupil: Because I find your classes so absorbing!

**What is a polygon?**
A dead parrot.

**Why was the math textbook miserable?**
It had too many problems.

**Why was the music teacher locked out of his classroom?**
The keys were on the piano.

**English teacher: Give me an example of a long sentence.**
Pupil: Life imprisonment.

**What did the pencil say to the protractor?**
Take me to your ruler.

**I sprained my ankle and had to miss gym for two weeks.**
Lucky you. Our gym teacher never accepts a lame excuse
for his class!

**Why don't leopards bother to cheat in exams?**
Because they know they will always be spotted!

# SCHOOL'S COOL

Is the math teacher in a good mood today?
I wouldn't count on it!

Teacher: Can you define the word "hardship"?
Silly pupil: Is it a boat made out of concrete?

My math teacher is a real peach!
You mean she's pretty?
No—I mean she has a heart of stone!

What do history teachers do before they get married?
They go out on dates!

Why is 6 afraid of 7?
Because 7 ate 9!

Parent: Why have you given my son such a bad grade in his report card? He's as intelligent as the next boy!
Teacher: Yes, but the next boy is an idiot!

Teacher: Eat up your school lunch—it's full of iron.
Pupil: That explains why it's so difficult to chew!

Teacher: How did people spend their time in the Stone Age?
Pupil: Did they listen to rock music?

Parent: Do you think my son has what it takes to become a pilot?
Teacher: Well, he certainly spends plenty of time with his head in the clouds!

**What happens when music teachers are sick?**
They send in a note!

**Why was the archeology teacher unhappy?**
Her career was in ruins.

**History teacher: How would you discover what life in Ancient Egypt was really like?**
Pupil: I'd ask my mummy!

**Did you hear about the math teacher whose mistakes started to multiply?**
In the end, they had to take him away!

**Why does your teacher have her hair in a bun?**
Because she has a face like a burger!

Teacher: What is the plural of baby?
Pupil: Twins!

Why do kindergarten teachers have such a positive attitude?
They know how to make the little things count.

Parent: Do you think my son will make a good Arctic explorer?
Teacher: I would think so: most of his grades are below zero!

Teacher: Can you tell me what water is?
Pupil: It's a colorless liquid that turns black when I put my hands in it!

Why is that boy locked up in a cage in the corner of the classroom?
Oh, he's the teacher's pet!

I think our school must be haunted.
Why?
Because the principal keeps talking about the school spirit!

Teacher: Who discovered Pluto?
Pupil: Walt Disney!

Teacher: What do Attila the Hun and Winnie the Pooh have in common?
Pupil: They have the same middle name!

Teacher: Michael, how do we know that the Earth is round?
Michael: I didn't say it was, Mr Johnson!

Teacher: If you multiply 245 by 3,456 and divide the answer by 165, then subtract 752, what will you get?
Pupil: The wrong answer!

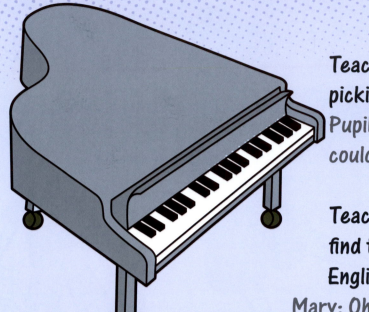

**Teacher: How good are you at picking up music?**
Pupil: Well, I'm not sure if I could lift a whole piano!

**Teacher: Mary, how did you find the questions in your English test?**
Mary: Oh, I found the questions easily enough—it's the answers I couldn't find!

**Teacher: Please don't talk while you are doing your exam.**
Pupil: It's all right, Miss Brown. We're not doing the exam—just talking!

**Teacher: Who invented fractions?**
Pupil: Henry the Eighth!

**Where do vampire schoolchildren go for field trips?**
Lake Eerie!

How does a math teacher remove hard wax from his ears?
He works it out with a pencil!

Teacher: Why were you late this morning, Veronica?
Veronica: I squeezed the toothpaste too hard, and it took me half an hour to get it all back into the tube again!

Pupil: Can we do some work on the Iron Age today?
Teacher: Well, I'm not certain, I'm a bit rusty on that period of history!

Ten cats were at the movies. One walked out. How many were left?
None—they were all copycats!

Teacher: What's a computer byte?
Pupil: I didn't even know they had teeth!

What happened after the wheel was first invented?
It caused a revolution!

Teacher: Did you know that most accidents happen in the kitchen?
Pupil: Yes, but we still have to eat them!

Mom: Time to get up and go to school!
Son: I don't want to go! Everyone hates me and I get bullied!
Mom: But you have to go – you're the principal!

Teacher: How many seconds are there in a year?
Pupil: Twelve—January 2nd, February 2nd...

What did the music teacher need a ladder for?
Reaching the high notes!

I banged my head on the locker door this morning!
Have you seen the school nurse?
No, just stars!

Teacher: Why is your homework late, young man?
Pupil: Sorry, Miss Elliot, my dad is a slow writer!

How do archeologists get into locked tombs, young man?
Do they use a skeleton key, Mr Edwards?

Math teacher: What are net profits?
Pupil: What fishermen have left after paying the crew!

I'm not really interested in math: I just go along to the lesson to make up the numbers!

What was the blackbird doing in the school library?
Looking for bookworms!

Did you hear about the gym teacher who used to run around the classroom in order to jog pupils' memories?

Why did the school orchestra have such awful manners?
Because it didn't know how to conduct itself!

Teacher: In the future, all trains and buses will run on time.
Pupil: Won't they run on fuel, just like now?

**Teacher: I wish you'd pay a little attention!**
Pupil: I'm paying as little as I can!

**Teacher: How did people react when electricity was first discovered?**
Pupil: They got a nasty shock!

**Young man, I hope I don't catch you cheating in the math test!**
So do I, Miss Goldman!

**What is a science teacher's favorite breed of dog?**
A lab!

**When do 2 and 2 make more than 4?**
When they make 22!

**Sign outside the music department:**
Violin for sale. Good price— no strings attached!

Teacher: Why was the invention of the safety match an important change?
Pupil: It was a striking achievement!

Why did the school cafeteria hire a dentist?
To make more filling meals!

Parent: Do you think my son could work as a DJ on the radio?
Teacher: He certainly has the face for it!

Why are teachers always welcome in pool halls?
Because they always bring their own chalk!

How do you know your school bus is old?
The seats are covered in mammoth hide!

Why did the burglar
break into the music
department?
He was after the lute!

Why was Cinderella
terrible at sports?
Because her coach
was a pumpkin!

Did you hear about the
math teacher and the
art teacher who used to go out together?
They spent their time painting by numbers!

Teacher: This homework looks as though it has been
written by your father.
Pupil: Of course it does—I borrowed his pen!

Teacher: Which two words in the English language have
the most letters?
Pupil: "Post Office!"

Teacher: Where were all the kings and queens of France crowned?
Pupil: On the head!

Teacher: Which age did the mummies live in?
Pupil: The Band-Age!

Where did King Arthur's men get their training?
At knight school!

What were the 16 schoolboys playing in the telephone booth?
Squash!

What sort of ring is always square?
A boxing ring!

# SiLLY SAFARi

# SILLY SAFARI

What did the blue whale say when he crashed into the bottlenose dolphin?
"I didn't do it on porpoise."

Where do reindeer run round and round in circles?
In Lapland.

What side of a porcupine is the sharpest?
The outside.

What do you call a giraffe with one leg?
Eileen.

Why did the lion spit out the clown?
Because he tasted funny.

**What did the tiger eat after he'd had all his teeth pulled out?**
The dentist.

**What do you call a sheep with no legs?**
A cloud.

**Why do giraffes have such long necks?**
Because they have very smelly feet.

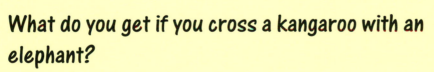

**What do you get if you cross a kangaroo with an elephant?**
Very big holes in your lawn.

**What do you call someone who lives with a pack of wolves?**
Wolfgang.

# SILLY SAFARI

**What does an octopus wear in the winter?**
A coat of arms.

**What do you call an elephant in a phone booth?**
Stuck.

**Where do sharks come from?**
Finland.

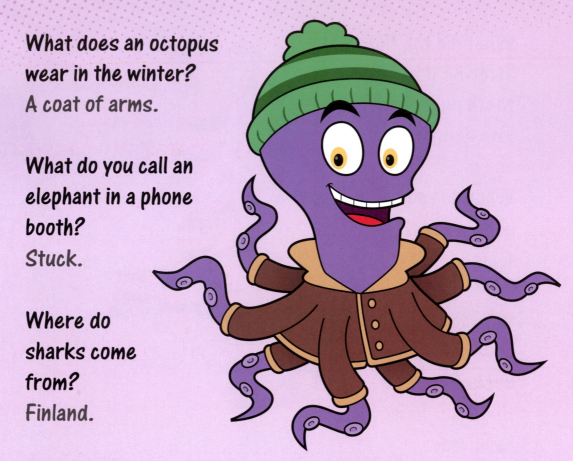

**What's the difference between a fish and a piano?**
You can't tuna fish!

**Why do insects hum?**
Because they can never remember the words!

**What's the best way to catch a fish?**
Get someone to throw it at you.

# SILLY SAFARI

**What's black and white and red all over?**
A sunburned penguin!

**What do you get if you cross a crocodile with a camera?**
A snapshot!

**Where are elephants found?**
They're so huge, it's quite difficult to lose them in the first place.

**Why wasn't the girl scared when a shark swam past her?**
She'd been told it was a man-eater.

**What's an elephant's favorite game?**
Squash.

A police officer saw a man walking down the street with a penguin. He told the man to take the penguin to the zoo.

"Good idea," the man said, and off he went.

The next day, the police officer saw the man again. He still had the penguin with him.

"I told you to take that penguin to the zoo," the police officer said.

"I did," the man replied. "He really enjoyed that, so today I'm taking him to the movies."

First leopard: Hey, is that a jogger over there?

Second leopard: Yes, great, I love fast food!

What do you get if you cross a snake with a bird?

A feather boa constrictor!

What's gray, has four legs, and a trunk?

A mouse going on vacation.

**What did the short-sighted porcupine say to the cactus?**
"Ah, there you are, dad!"

**What do penguins do in their spare time?**
They chill.

**Spotted in the library:**
*I Fell Down a Rabbit Hole* by Alison Wonderland.

**What do you call a dead skunk?**
Ex-stinked!

**Why was the mother firefly sad?**
Because her children weren't very bright!

**What is the best thing to do when a hippo sneezes?**
Get out of the way!

# SILLY SAFARI

What lives in a
forest and tells
the dullest
stories ever
heard?
A wild boar!

What did the
silliest kid in
school call
his pet zebra?
"Spot!"

What would you do if a
jellyfish stung you?
I'd break every bone in its body!

What does a frog use to put up shelves?
A toad's tool!

How did the fruit bats go into Noah's Ark?
In pears!

# SILLY SAFARI

**Why are hyenas always falling out?**
They always have a bone to pick with each other!

**What are the scariest dinosaurs?**
Terror dactyls!

**What do you call a criminal bird?**
An illegal eagle!

**What sort of fish would you find in a bird cage?**
A perch!

**What sort of horses do monsters ride?**
Night mares!

# SILLY SAFARI

**Why was the zebra put in charge of the jungle army?**
Because he had the most stripes!

**How do you catch a squirrel?**
Climb a tree and act like a nut.

**What's big, furry, and flies?**
A hot-air baboon.

**How do you stop moles from digging up your lawn?**
Hide the shovels.

**What's the difference between a crazy rabbit and a counterfeit ten-dollar bill?**
One's a mad bunny and the other's bad money.

**What sea creatures do you find on legal documents?**
Seals.

**Why should you never trust a whale with your deepest, darkest secrets?**
Because they're all blubbermouths.

**Where do camels keep their money?**
In sand banks.

**Where do tadpoles change into frogs?**
In a croakroom.

**What sort of animal will never oversleep?**
A llama clock!

# SILLY SAFARI

**What do rhinoceroses have that no other animal has?**
Baby rhinoceroses.

**What do you get if you cross an angry sheep with a mad cow?**
An animal that's in a baaaaaaaaaaaaaaad moooooooooooooood.

**Why can't leopards hide from hunters?**
Because they are always spotted!

**When do kangaroos propose marriage?**
In leap years!

**Where do rabbits learn to fly?**
In the Hare Force!

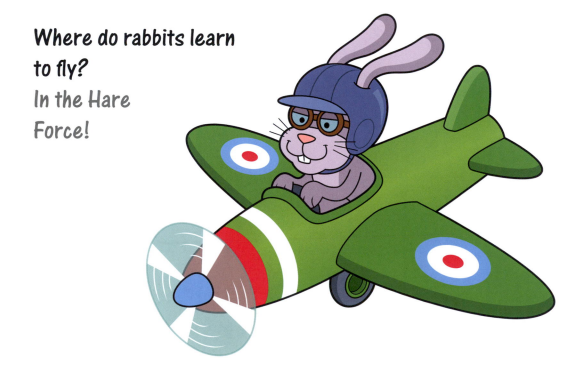

# SILLY SAFARI

Did you hear
about the
spiders who got
married?
They had a huge
webbing.

What job did the
spider get?
Web designer!

What do you call
a worm in a fur
coat?
A caterpillar!

What do you call a bad-tempered bee?
A grumblebee.

Doctor, I think I'm a frog.
So what's the problem?
I'm sure I'm going to croak.

**What do you get if you cross a dinosaur with a fish?**
Jurassic shark!

**What do you call a phone for alligators?**
A croco-dial!

**Did you hear about the wizard who made honey?**
He was a spelling bee!

**What do you call pigs who write to each other?**
Pen pals!

**How do elephants travel?**
In jumbo jets!

# SILLY SAFARI

**What do camels wear when they play hide-and-seek?**
Camel-flage.

**What is a porpoise's favorite TV show?**
Whale of Fortune.

**What do you get if you cross a sheep with a bucket of water?**
A wet blanket.

**What did the rabbit say when it went bald?**
Hare today, gone tomorrow!

**Which bird is always out of breath?**
A puffin.

# SiLLY SAFARi

Why do sick crabs walk sideways?
Because their medicine has side-effects!

What should you do if you see a blue whale?
Try to cheer him up.

What did the celebrity squirrels sign before
they got married?
A pre-nutshell agreement.

How can you tell if there's an elephant in the refrigerator?
You can't shut the door!

Why did the elephant refuse
to play cards with his
two friends?
Because one of them
was lion and the
other was a
cheetah!

# SILLY SAFARI

What do you call an owl who robs the rich and gives to the poor?
Robin Hoot!

What do toads say when they greet each other?
"Wart's new with you?"

What is a goat's favorite food?
Alpha-butt soup!

What do you get if you cross a leopard and a bunch of flowers?
A beauty spot!

Doctor, I think I'm a crocodile!
Don't worry—you'll soon snap out of it!

How do you get around on the seabed?
By taxi-crab!

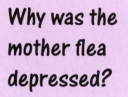

What went into the lion's cage at the zoo and came out without a scratch?
Another lion!

Why was the mother flea depressed?
All her children had gone to the dogs!

How do you know if there's an elephant in your refrigerator?
Look for footprints in the butter!

How do you get down from a camel?
You don't. You get down from a goose.

# SILLY SAFARI

**How do you stop a rhinoceros from charging?**
Take away its cash register.

**What happened to the shark who swallowed a bunch of keys?**
He got lockjaw!

**Which animal was out of bounds?**
The exhausted kangaroo.

**What do you give a deaf fish?**
A herring aid.

**What do you call a hippo at the South Pole?**
Lost!

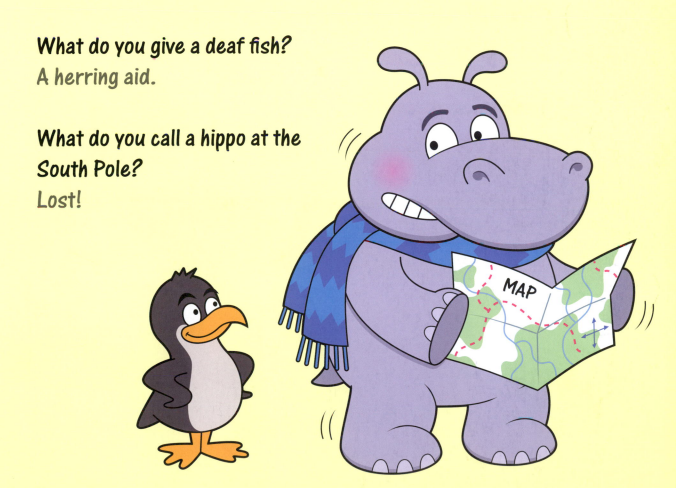

## SILLY SAFARI

What do you get if you cross a snake with a builder?
A boa constructor.

Where does a blackbird go for a drink?
To a crowbar.

What do porcupines say when they hug?
"Ouch!"

What do you get if you cross a fish with an elephant?
Swimming trunks.

What do you call
a monkey who
is king of the
jungle?
Henry the Ape!